THE STORY OF JESUS

by
Mary McMillan

illus*
Bron Smith

Cover by Dan Grossm:

Shining Star Publicatio   Copyright © 1988
A Division of Good A   , Inc.

ISBN No. 0-86653-454

Standardized Subject C   TA ac

Printing No. 9876543

Shining Star Publicat
A Division of Good A   e, Inc.
Box 299
Carthage, IL 62321-

Unless otherwise indicated, the King James Version of the Bible was used in preparing the activities in this book.

Shining Star Publications, Copyright © 1988, A division of Good Apple, Inc.   SS1804

TABLE OF CONTENTS

Shining Star Publications, Copyright © 1988, A division of Good Apple, Inc.

SS1804

TEACHING TIPS

This book has been created to educate as well as entertain young children. The purpose of this book is to familiarize children with THE STORY OF JESUS and to teach size. BIG/little, HUGE/tiny, TALL/short, and LARGE/small are introduced and reinforced in the sticker story and cut-and-paste projects.

Make sure the children understand the task that is to be completed before they begin. Study the illustration showing the completed project and have the children verbalize the steps they must follow. They will need scissors, paste*, crayons, a hole punch, string, tissue paper in several different colors, 1 dowel rod (25″ long), 15 pieces of construction paper, felt material for banner if available (paper can be substituted), and 1 shoe box to complete the project. Children should be familiar with the direction codes used on each page. Explain that a solid dark line indicates where to cut. Dotted lines are to be folded up and dashes mean to fold down. Small circles indicate where to use the hole punch.

Children develop many learning skills at an early age, and you can help youngsters increase their readiness skills with the activities in this book. When working with young children, praise and encourage each accomplishment. Thinking and planning are more important than the neatness of the finished page.

This collection of practical cut-and-paste projects will encourage youngsters to develop eye-hand coordination. The story about Jesus' life will give children an opportunity to experience success and build self-esteem as they become involved in learning new skills.

*You can make the stickers for this book ready for the children to attach to the pages by the following method.

1. Mix equal amounts of Elmer's or Lepage's Mucilage and water together in a small container (paper cup).
2. Use a paintbrush and apply the glue mixture to the back of each sticker page.
3. Let the pages dry completely, glue side up. After the children cut out the stickers, let them dampen the back of the prepared stickers with a lightly wet sponge or brush.

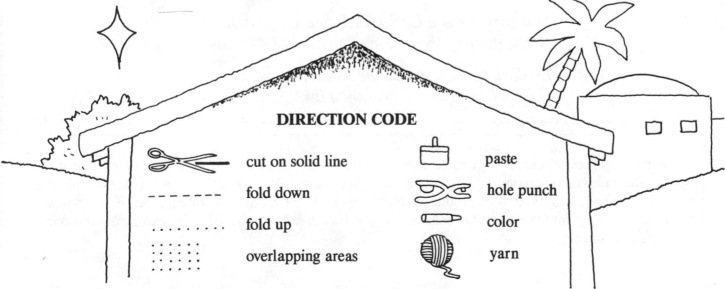

DIRECTION CODE

✂	cut on solid line	🪣	paste
- - - - -	fold down	✄	hole punch
. . . . . .	fold up	▭	color
⦂⦂⦂⦂	overlapping areas	🧶	yarn

···· THE STORY OF JESUS ····

Stars in the heavens were shining that night.
Wise men and shepherds were awed by the sight.

A small tiny babe had been placed on the hay
In a stable where donkeys and cows also lay.

In the temple of God He was blessed and was named
Jesus, God's Son, whom the angels proclaimed!

Joseph went home with his wife and his boy.
In Galilee all of them shared such great joy.

Jesus was thoughtful. With never a shrug,
He'd help His dear mother with each heavy jug.

Careful with each of the carpenter's tools,
The young lad watched father make wagons and stools.

At twelve He amazed all the learned and wise:
He taught from the Bible—what a surprise!

With a blink of an eye and a nod of the head,
He soon grew to manhood, and God's word He spread.

Teaching and preaching and healing the blind,
He cared for the sick; to all He was kind.

Down by the seashore, disciples He found,
Fishing from boats, making nets on the ground.

They took Jesus' message to rich and to poor.
They spoke in the market, in streets, at the door.

In a dark garden Christ knelt and He prayed
While three of them slept. The atonement* was made.

He died, but arose—all the world to forgive!
If we follow Him, we also shall live!

---

*The term atonement could be a discussion lesson wherein the explanation might be offered that Jesus paid for the mistakes everyone else made or will ever make. He "atoned" for us. For example, "If you broke someone's toy and your mother or father paid for the broken toy or replaced it, they would have PAID for your mistake." Similar examples might be offered that would help young children relate to this difficult concept.

SS1804

Put the LITTLE star in the LITTLE circle.

LITTLE

Sticker on page 19.

BIG

Sticker on page 19.

Put the BIG star in the BIG circle.

Stars in the heavens were shining that night.
Wise men and shepherds were awed by the sight.

SS1804

Put HIM next to the lamb.

Put HER beside the donkey.

HIM

Sticker on page 19.

HER

Sticker on page 19.

A small tiny babe had been placed on the hay
In a stable where donkeys and cows also lay.

SS1804

Put a star on the OUTSIDE of the temple.

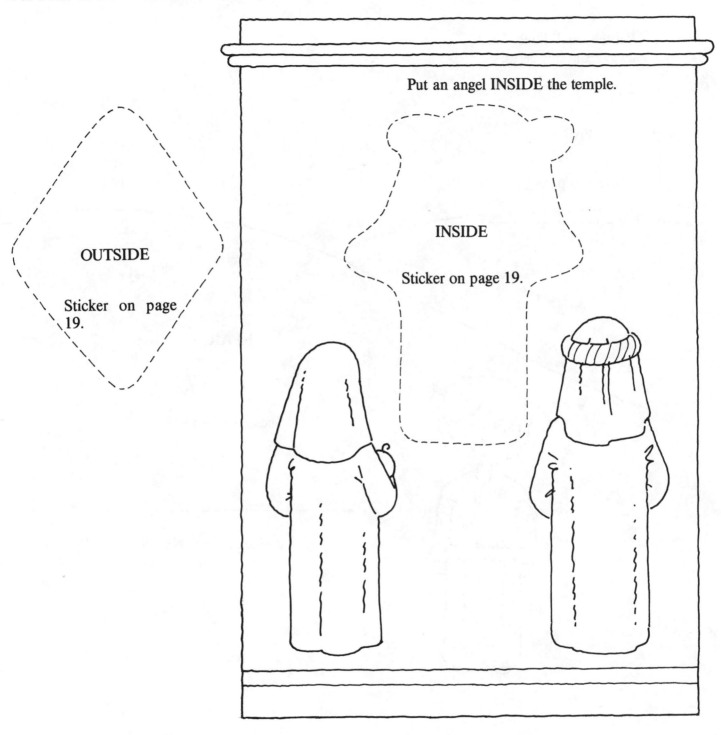

Put an angel INSIDE the temple.

OUTSIDE

Sticker on page 19.

INSIDE

Sticker on page 19.

In the temple of God He was blessed and was named Jesus, God's Son, whom the angels proclaimed!

SS1804

Put the small house FAR
away from boy Jesus.

FAR

Sticker on page 19.

NEAR

Sticker on page 19.

Put the large house NEAR
boy Jesus.

Joseph went home with his wife and his boy.
In Galilee all of them shared such great joy.

SS1804

Put one water jug ON the table.

ON

Sticker on page 19.

OFF

Sticker on
page 19.

Put one water jug OFF to the
side of the table.

Jesus was thoughtful. With never a shrug,
He'd help His dear mother with each heavy jug.

SS1804

Put the wagon at the TOP of the page.

TOP

Sticker on page 21.

BOTTOM

Sticker on page 21.

Put the stool at the BOTTOM of the page.

Careful with each of the carpenter's tools,
The young lad watched father make wagons and stools.

SS1804

Put the OLD man beside boy Jesus.

OLD

Sticker on page 21.

Sticker on page 21.

YOUNG

Put the YOUNG man beside the other men.

At twelve He amazed all the learned and wise:
He taught from the Bible—what a surprise!

SS1804

Put the boy Jesus on the
LEFT side of the star.

Put the man Jesus on the
RIGHT side of the star.

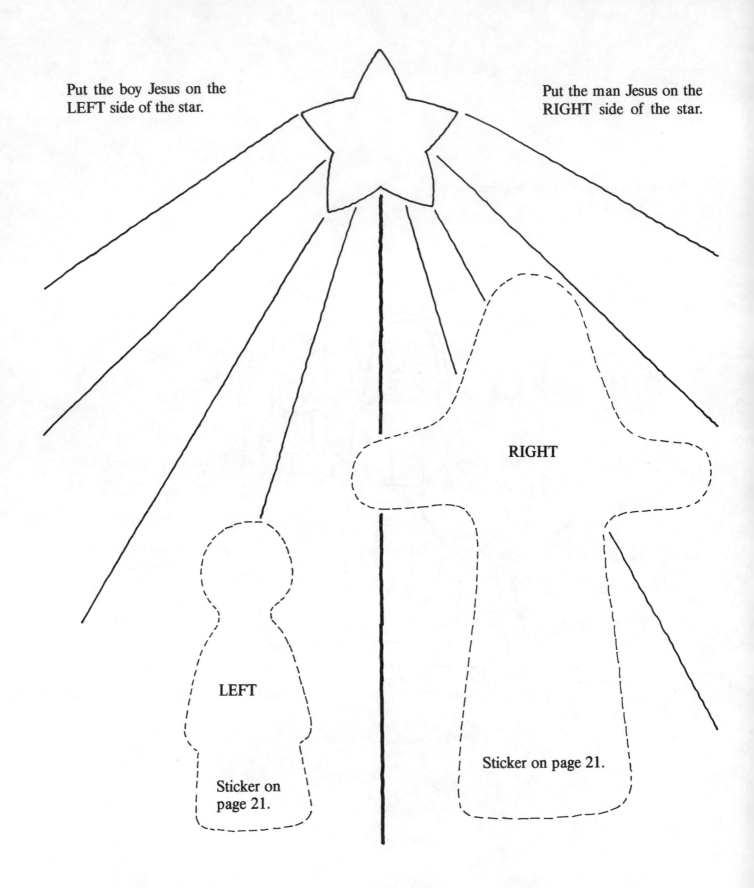

RIGHT

LEFT

Sticker on page 21.

Sticker on
page 21.

With a blink of an eye and a nod of the head,
He soon grew to manhood, and God's word He spread.

SS1804

Put the cloud ABOVE the crowd.

ABOVE

Sticker on page 21.

BELOW

Sticker on page 21.

Put the donkey BELOW the crowd.

Teaching and preaching and healing the blind,
He cared for the sick; to all He was kind.

SS1804

BACK
Sticker on page 23.

Put the crab in BACK of Jesus.

Put the shell in FRONT of Jesus.

FRONT

Sticker on page 23.

Down by the seashore, disciples He found,
Fishing from boats, making nets on the ground.

SS1804

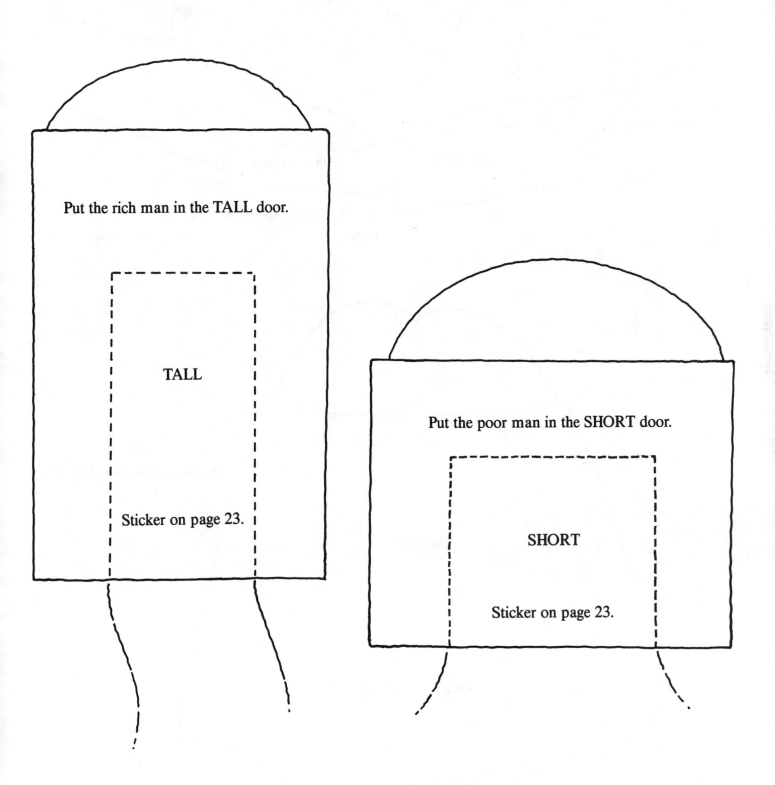

Put the rich man in the TALL door.

TALL

Sticker on page 23.

Put the poor man in the SHORT door.

SHORT

Sticker on page 23.

They took Jesus' message to rich and to poor.
They spoke in the market, in streets, at the door.

SS1804

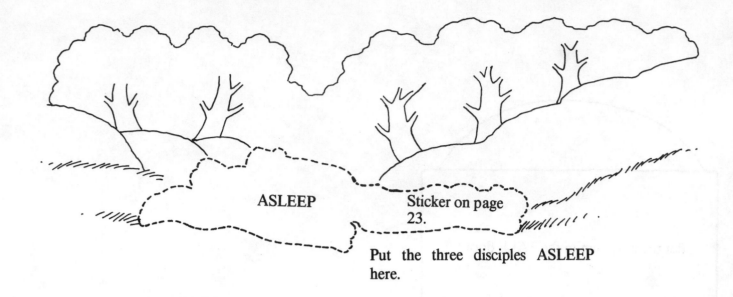

ASLEEP

Sticker on page 23.

Put the three disciples ASLEEP here.

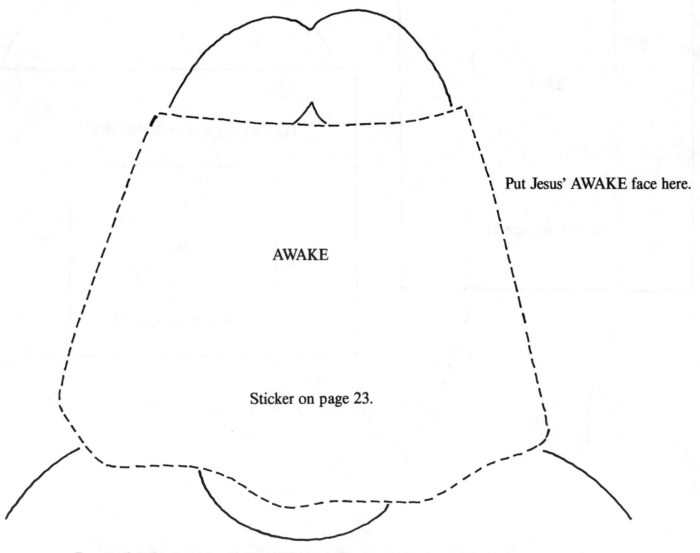

Put Jesus' AWAKE face here.

AWAKE

Sticker on page 23.

In a dark garden Christ knelt and He prayed
While three of them slept. The atonement* was made.

*See page 4.

SS1804

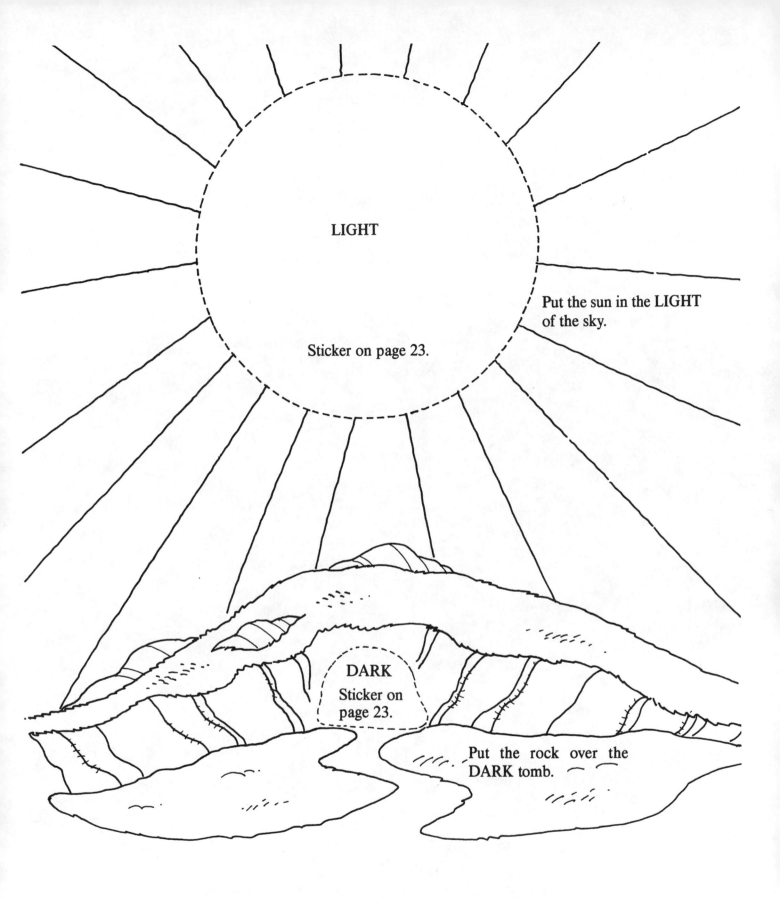

LIGHT

Sticker on page 23.

Put the sun in the LIGHT of the sky.

DARK
Sticker on page 23.

Put the rock over the DARK tomb.

He died, but arose—all the world to forgive!
If we follow Him, we also shall live!

SS1804

18

STICKERS FOR PAGES 5-9

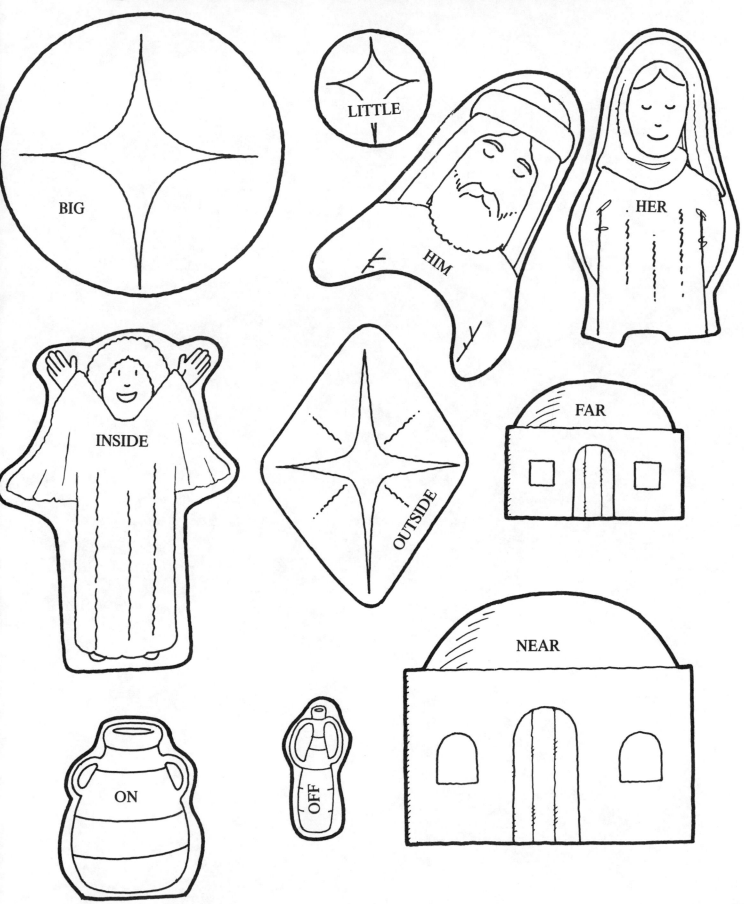

BIG

LITTLE

HIM

HER

INSIDE

OUTSIDE

FAR

NEAR

ON

OFF

SS1804

STICKERS FOR PAGES 10-13

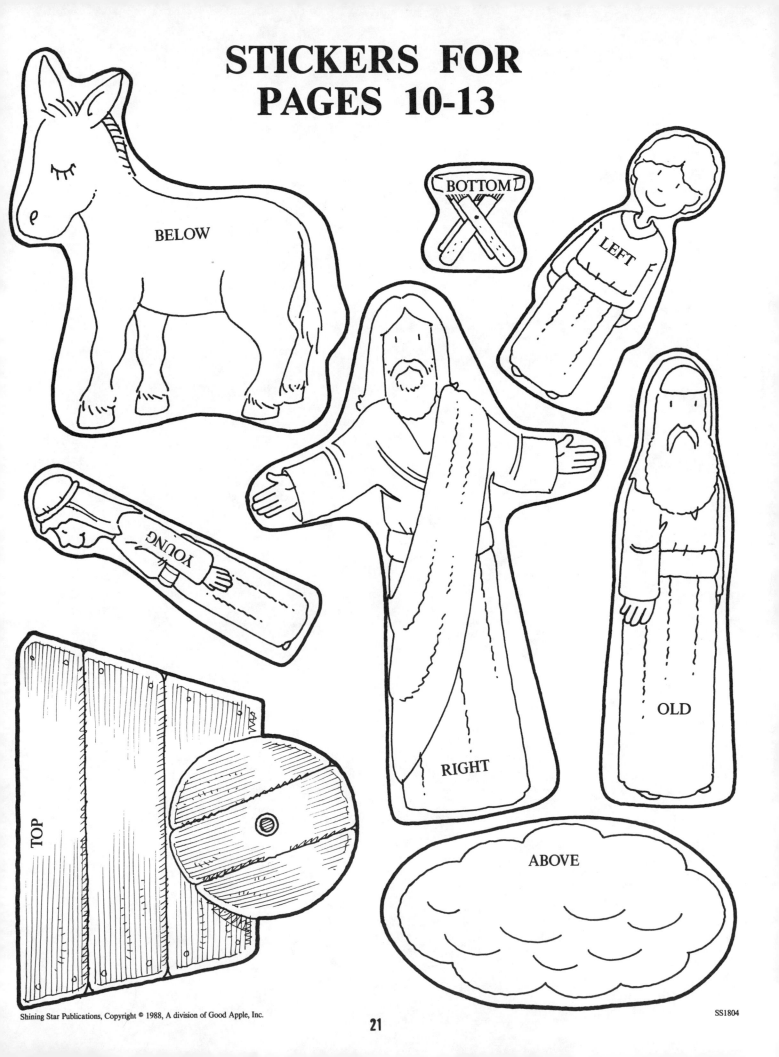

BELOW

BOTTOM

LEFT

YOUNG

RIGHT

OLD

TOP

ABOVE

SS1804

STICKERS FOR PAGES 14-17

FRONT

BACK

TALL

SHORT

ASLEEP

AWAKE

LIGHT

DARK

SS1804

A CHRISTMAS ORNAMENT

Stars in the heavens were shining that night
Wise men and shepherds were awed by the sight.

A small tiny babe had been placed on the hay
In a stable where donkeys and cows also lay.

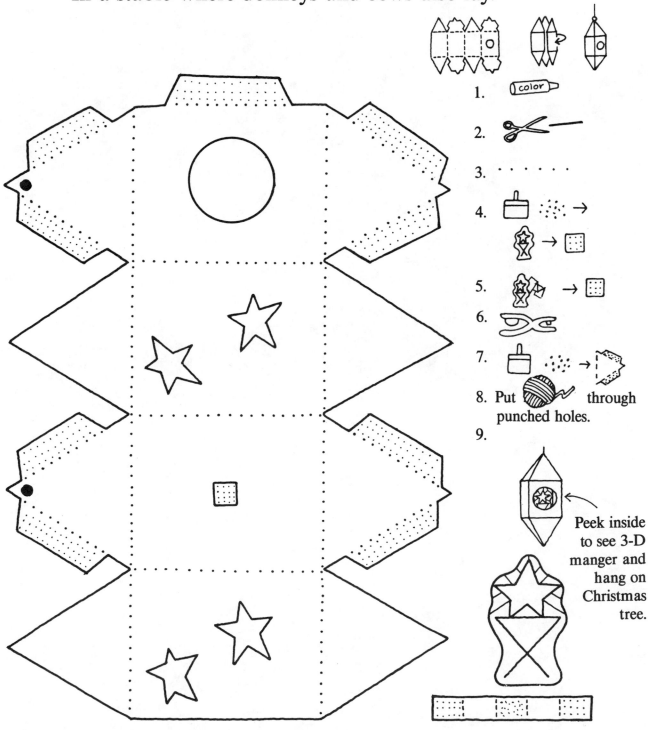

1.
2.
3. · · · · ·
4.
5.
6.
7.
8. Put   through punched holes.
9.

Peek inside to see 3-D manger and hang on Christmas tree.

SS1804

THE TEMPLE'S STAINED-GLASS WINDOW

In the temple of God He was blessed and was named
Jesus, God's Son, whom the angels proclaimed!

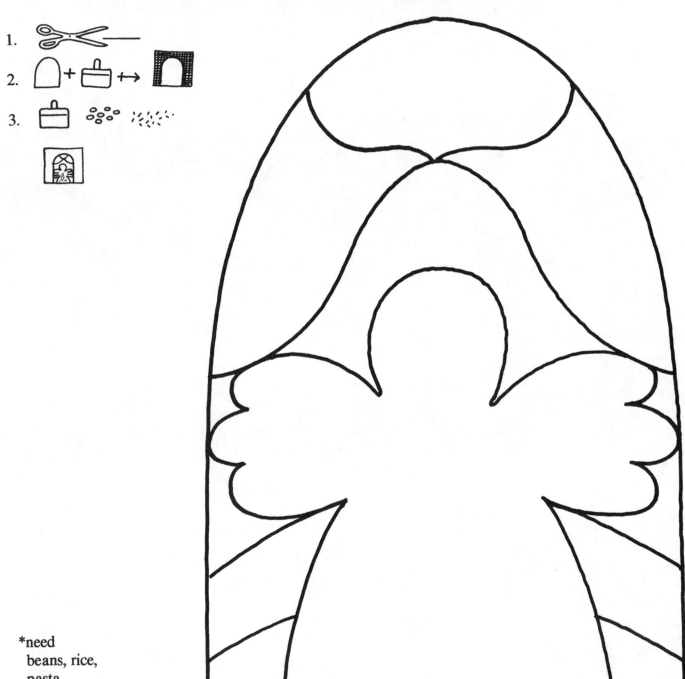

1.

2.

3.

*need
beans, rice,
pasta,
small
pieces of
colored
paper, etc.

SS1804

STAND-UP WATER JUG

Jesus was thoughtful. With never a shrug,
    He'd help His dear mother with each heavy jug.

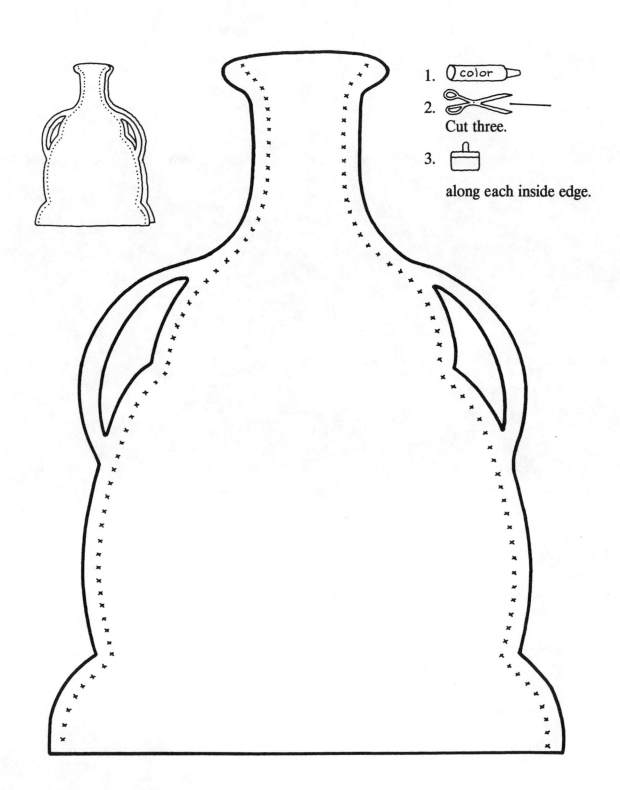

1. color
2. Cut three.
3. along each inside edge.

JOSEPH'S SAW/JESUS' SANDALS

Careful with each of the carpenter's tools,
The young lad watched father make wagons and stools.

At twelve He amazed all the learned and wise:
He taught from the Bible—what a surprise!

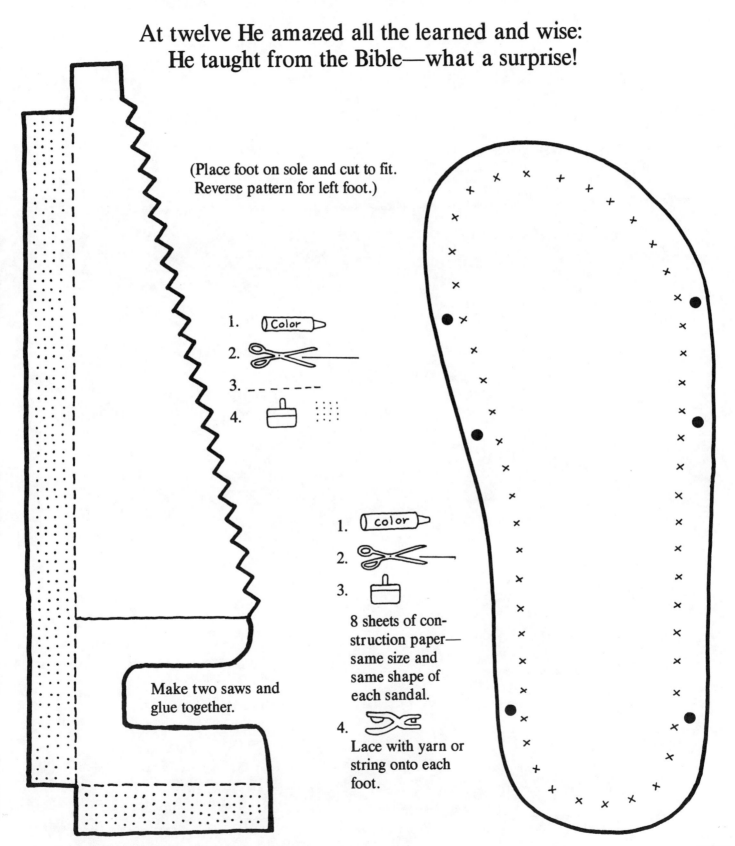

(Place foot on sole and cut to fit.
Reverse pattern for left foot.)

1. Color
2. ✂
3. - - - - -
4.

1. Color
2. ✂
3.

8 sheets of con-
struction paper—
same size and
same shape of
each sandal.

4.
Lace with yarn or
string onto each
foot.

Make two saws and
glue together.

SS1804

PATTERNS FOR BANNER

With a blink of an eye and a nod of the head,
He soon grew to manhood, and God's word He spread.

Materials and Instructions

Use paper, burlap, felt or other appropriate material for background. ("Mom, I'll need your help here!")
Size—24" x 48".
Sew, or glue, ¾" seam at top.
Insert dowel rod through top.
Tie string to each end of rod and hang on wall.
Cut out patterns and glue or sew onto banner.

1. Color

2. (scissors)

3. (glue)

SS1804

PATTERNS FOR BANNER
(Cont'd.)

SS1804

DOCTOR'S KIT

Teaching and preaching and healing the blind,
He cared for the sick; to all He was kind.

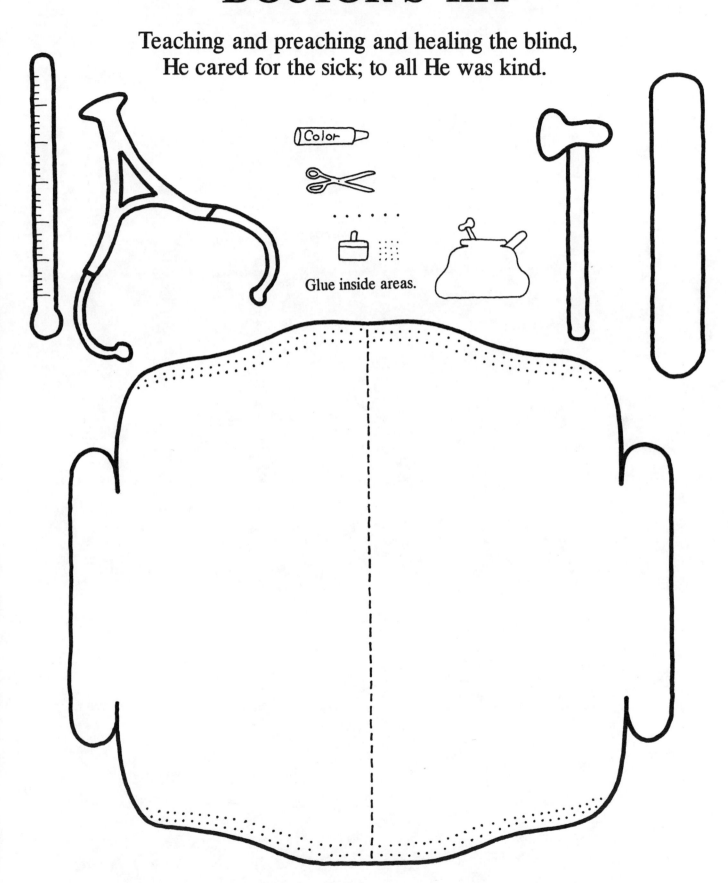

Glue inside areas.

SS1804

SEASHORE AQUARIUM

Down by the seashore, disciples He found,
Fishing from boats, making nets on the ground.

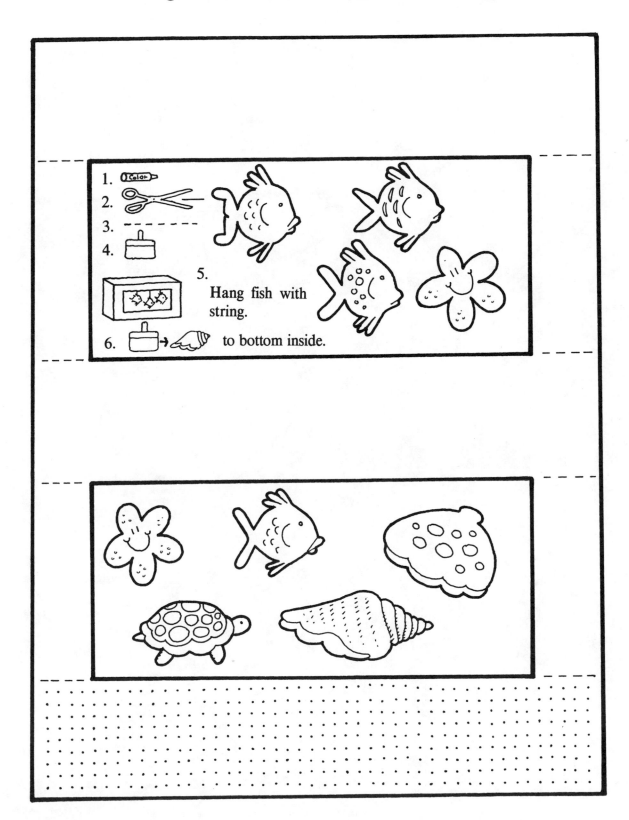

5. Hang fish with string.

6. to bottom inside.

SS1804

PICK-A-DOOR ELEVATOR

They took Jesus' message to rich and to poor.
They spoke in the market, in streets, at the door.

1. Color   2. [scissors]   3. - - - - - -   4. [glue] [dots]

Outside of elevator →

ELEVATOR

→

Going down

ELEVATOR

←

Going up

ELEVATOR

←

Going up

→

Going down

ELEVATOR

 SS1804

PICK-A-DOOR ELEVATOR
(Cont'd.)

1.  Color   2. ✄   3. - - - - - -   4. ▭ ⋮⋮⋮

Inside of elevator ↘

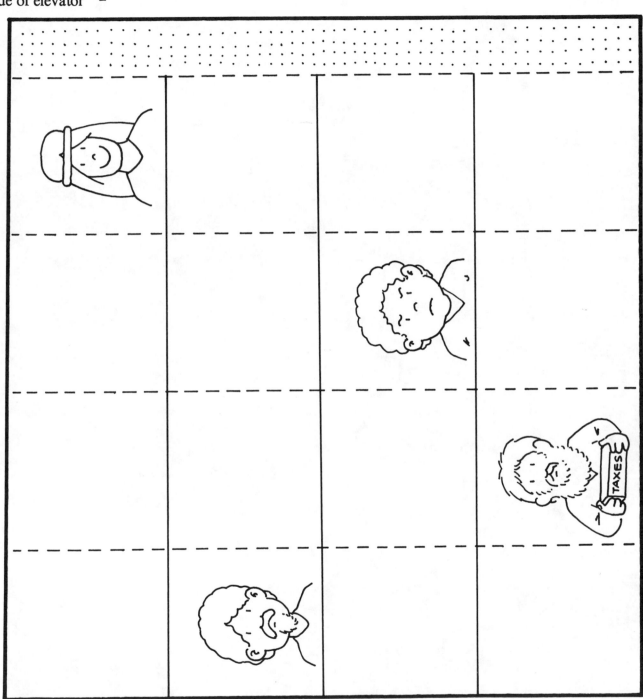

SS1804

CHRIST AROSE
SHADOW BOX

In a dark garden Christ knelt and He prayed
  While three of them slept, the atonement* was made.

He died, but arose—all the world to forgive!
  If we follow Him, we also shall live!

Materials:
One shoe box

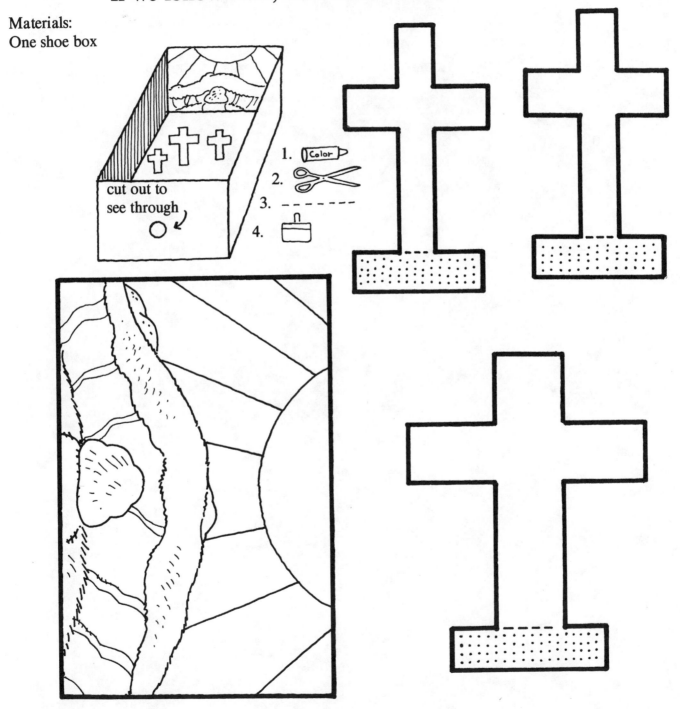

1. Color
2. ✂
3. - - - - -
4.

cut out to
see through

*See page 4.

SS1804